It's Not Too Late To Be Great!
My Story of Recovery

It's Not Too Late To Be Great!

MY STORY OF RECOVERY

NICKY SEWELL

StoryTerrace

Text Jenny Firth-Cozens, on behalf of StoryTerrace

Design StoryTerrace

Copyright © Nicky Sewell

First print February 2022

StoryTerrace

www.StoryTerrace.com

CONTENTS

1. A BOW CHILDHOOD — 7
2. THE EARLY ROLE OF ALCOHOL DISCOVERY — 25
3. THE DOWNWARD SLIDE — 39
4. THE DARK, DARK PLACE – AND LIGHT — 43
5. LIFE IN AA — 51
6. THE STEPS TO FEELING GREAT — 61

1

A BOW CHILDHOOD

I look back on my childhood with real pleasure. It had plenty of affection and fun, and none of the unhappiness that some children suffer. I loved my parents and I felt loved by them.

We lived in a council house in Bow, in the East End of London. My dad had been a fireman during World War II. He'd been on duty during some of the worst raids of the Blitz on London. His older brothers had both been killed in France in the First World War, so his mother must have been grateful to have him home, though being a fireman was extremely dangerous. After the war he became a porter at Billingsgate fish market.

Dad had been married before, to a Jewish woman who had died young leaving him with three children. Perhaps my mum was attracted to someone she saw as a real 'man's man'. He worked hard, supporting six children, but enjoyed the pub and playing darts. She married him and had my sister, then me and, eight years later, my younger brother.

Me at the flat where I lived

My home in Bow, now refurbished

Dad in the fire brigade, wearing a white shirt with the sleeves rolled up

Dad's Fish Porter badge at Billingsgate

So I grew up one of six, though three of them were much older than me with children of their own.

My father was a strong figure in our lives and there's no doubt he was happiest when he knew we were doing the right thing, and would let us know in no uncertain terms if we weren't! He loved sport and would come and watch me, and later my brother, playing football. My brother was very good and, as a young player, was on the books of Orient, Crystal Palace and Tottenham.

My mother was a remarkable woman. She looked after us all and kept us and the house in order, but she also ran the local tenants' association and was involved in a charity: The East End Charity for Under-Privileged East End Children, linked to Kingsley Hall, a wonderful community centre that is continuing in Dagenham. Richard Attenborough was the Patron and he would come to tea with us, his Rolls Royce parked incongruously outside. Kingsley Hall has been active since 1929. Gandhi chose to stay there in the thirties and my dad, a good athlete and representing the London School-Boys Association, met him there. My mother was certainly well-loved for all the work she did. She died when I was twenty-seven and a thousand people came to her funeral.

I believe I enjoyed all the things you might expect for a child growing up in that East End community. There were holidays on the Isle of Wight, collecting all the different colours of sand you can find there, and others on the Isle

Me and my sister Janet on holiday by the sea on the Isle of Wight

of Sheppey, flying kites and building sandcastles. I am still happiest by the sea.

As youngsters, we could get on a Red Bus Rover and spend a whole day travelling all over London, often with the adventure of getting lost when we got off somewhere strange. I remember the joy of having a toffee-apple man selling toffee-apples from his motorbike, even coconut-covered ones. My neighbour's dog would chase him down the street.

There was a local wood mill close by with piles of discarded timber out the back and I would make shields and swords and my mate would paint them amazingly well so we could have battles together. We made go-carts and played knock-down ginger and cannon: tying cotton to a door knocker, pulling it so it knocked and the owner came to the door. Then doing it all again till they shouted.

Although money was tight, the socialist principles of the local politics meant I was given grants to have holidays with the school and so I went to Italy skiing on four occasions. I could ski quite well by the end of those.

Things changed when I was ten and dad lost his job and only had the rag-and-bone business, so the family income went down fast. He'd worked there all his life and, understandably, it was a big upset for him and for all of us. He was fifty-eight by then and mum was forty-six.

As a teenager, I worked Saturdays at a cigarette lighter stall in Petticoat Lane and I restocked the shelves of the

Me on a skiing trip with school, I'm in the middle

local pub over the weekend. Unfortunately they had a large guard dog which would sometimes stop me getting up the stairs from the cellar so I could be stuck down there until the bottles ran out above! During school holidays I'd help my dad on the rag-and-bone cart which he drove round after his early mornings at Billingsgate. We would travel all around London picking up old clothes and household items. When we got home, we would sort it all out in the hallway of our house, which made an incredible mess. I would not invite anyone around the house because of the embarrassment of the mess.

Needless to say, I wasn't always a good boy, so I managed by accident to burn down two local shops when I built the biggest Guy Fawkes' bonfire anyone had ever seen. My little brother wasn't much better when it came to fire, and our house burnt down completely when he played with the paraffin heater, so we had to live with my nan while the council rebuilt it, but that was all part of childhood.

Overall, I was a lucky child and things should have been good for me, but I was always anxious – worrying about my mum and dad, primarily because I was constantly terrified that they would die. I'd often have to stay in their room because some n'er-do-well was staying with us, like my uncle who was a friend of the Krays. I'd lay awake listening all the time to my parents' breathing to make sure they were still alive. It was probably because they were quite old for parents but in reality, I worried about everything.

IT'S NOT TOO LATE TO BE GREAT!

Not Good Enough

For some reason I could never just accept that anything about me was actually good. I always felt whatever I got or whatever I did was only second-best. For example, I was given a yellow Chopper bike – all the luckiest kids got one. Yellow was the traditional colour for a Chopper, but as soon as I got it, I wanted a red one; yellow just seemed wrong. I know if they'd given me red, I'd have wanted yellow, because that's what happened throughout my young life, and even later. When I became a London taxi-driver my friend said: 'Well done, Nicky!' I said: 'Yeah, but really I'd rather be a tipper driver.' Because *he* was a tipper driver! I compared myself constantly to other people and they felt 'right' to me, but I always felt 'wrong'. Later in my life I went through a stage of buying different Rolex watches, thinking that the more expensive they were, the happier I'd be. Such a fallacy!

Nowadays I explain the feeling of 'nothing's ever right' in this way: it's as if I have a new tee-shirt on, and yet never feel comfortable in it, as if it's inside-out or back-to-front. This feeling of discomfort existed as far back as I can remember – nothing ever felt good enough. For many years it was only alcohol that made me feel 'right' again.

The estate was large and there would be at least forty kids playing out at football and cricket and other sports. I would go out to play with them, but before I did I would ask Mum to call me in to help – so I would have an excuse to leave. This meant that I was washing up and hoovering instead of playing out.

I know now that this is very common for alcoholics – this out-of-place feeling, the sensation that nothing you do or have will be good enough. So everything we do is extreme – it's all or nothing. If I love, it's extreme; but also if I'd had a Porsche, I would wonder why it wasn't a Bugatti. Until I stopped drinking, I lived with the constant sensation that the more I had, the more I wanted: not from greed, but because having more never quite worked.

I know now that, in terms of alcoholics, we just have to make sure we don't have the first drink because we'll only want another and another: it will never quite work. There's some evidence now that this could have a physiological cause: that the feeling of 'the more I have, the more I want' actually comes from a different enzyme in the brains of addicts.

Despite feeling out of place so much of the time, I was captain of the football team and played at the district level for cricket. I'd even taken part in plays. So I got involved in lots of activities, but the feeling of isolation stayed with me and refused to go away – until I discovered alcohol.

However, it might not have all been negative: I am sure that, because I always felt not-good-enough, this actually gave me a strong drive to do better. This would generally be a good thing, but perhaps not on top of loneliness.

Eventually it became a driver for me to drink, as it is for many alcoholics. Now I'm sober, I use the same drive to help other people.

Adolescence

From secondary school on I had only one real friend, Danny, and I stuck to that. We were inseparable and went on holiday together with the school and down to his parents' caravan. Later on we'd go to pubs together. In my very darkest days he was very good to my wife, listening if she needed to talk, and was like a second father to my daughter Natalie. When she was seventeen, he even bought her her first car. He's been a very true friend to this day.

Back then, still at school, I looked very different. As a rather handsome teenager I had long blonde hair to swish around. But I was extremely shy and long hair might have been used as a bit of a curtain. Certainly girls liked me, but they would call me a snob because they said I wouldn't look at them, which was simply to do with my being so shy. I can still find it hard to look at people all the time when I talk to them.

At fourteen things were made worse for my self-esteem when I lost a finger. I'd been climbing over a fence with my mates, trying to get into a disco, when my ring-finger got caught in the wire and was torn off. The surgeon spelt out all the risks involved in trying to sew it back on – including losing my arm - and so I had to make a choice and I chose to lose it. Fourteen is a very self-conscious age anyway, but this only made it more extreme.

However, I have no doubt now that, if it wasn't the finger, it would have been something else. It was always a big thing for me as an adolescent but, in reality, the only thing that I've lost because of it was a job as a city trader – and that was because you can't make the finger-signals you need if you have one of them missing! People simply don't notice it: to such an extent that my wife and I had been together for four months when she bought me a ring for that finger!

My sister looked after me, and then, as I got older, I looked after her and stuck up for her when she needed it. She's a hard-worker and is involved in the charity arm of the company she works for in Canary Wharf. She's become the mother of the family and she's wonderful. My younger brother might have seen me as a bit of a bully when we were young because I was so much older, but we still did things together. He's done very well in his life and I love him very much.

I was always handy with my fists, and I'd use them to protect myself and others. Fighting was part of life in the East End. In school or in the pubs, there were always fights, especially as I was a West Ham supporter. I did have a temper, it's true, and sometimes I've definitely let it rip badly, but I would always prefer being a lover to being a fighter - having a good time and a chat with girls. The fights

Me and my sister on her wedding day

Me and my brother Jimmy at home

happened because it seemed like you had to as it was part of the culture – not otherwise. Later, when alcohol had taken over, the violence came more from jealousy or paranoid feelings.

It was a very different life then, growing up in the East End. The gangsters, the codes, the lack of forgiveness for transgressions against you. What was normal there is so different to where I am now in the Medway. People here put up with so much, things they certainly wouldn't stand for in Bow. There were not too many chances given where I grew up.

Me with my brother and sister at my niece Lucy's wedding in Cyprus

2

THE EARLY ROLE OF ALCOHOL DISCOVERY

I never wanted to drink. I went into pubs and I worked in them too: bottling up and as a DJ which I was surprisingly good at. But I'd just have juice. I was very sporty and this was one reason I chose not to drink or smoke, but also, I couldn't have coped with the embarrassment of being refused because I was too young.

I didn't drink alcohol till I was about sixteen. A barmaid, who was said not to question anyone's age, sold me a gin and orange. That seemed a very grown-up drink to me, and I was away.

From that night on I always felt that there was no point in having a drink unless it really altered how I felt. It was never a relaxant for me; I couldn't just have a drink to wind down after work. On the contrary, it made me want to hit the town. The more I drank, the more I buzzed in a way I loved. This was a very new sensation for me. Everything changed. I'd had lots of girls around me, but I'd been completely tongue-

Me and my mates out

Me in Tarzan fancy dress in London

tied so it never went very far. However, with a drink I'd be jumping on tables and even stripping. It didn't take much.

I've never been a falling-about drunk: something in my metabolism must stop that happening because it certainly didn't reflect the quantity I drank. However, it probably had an effect on the fights I somehow managed to get caught up in.

Starting Work

At sixteen I left school, like most of my class. No one I knew went on to university; no one became a doctor or a lawyer, but several were very entrepreneurial and had successful businesses or made money from crime. It wasn't that no one was clever enough; it was more that we knew no one who did that and nothing was expected of us. I got an apprenticeship as a design engineer in a heating company in the city with one day and one evening a week at college. At weekends I'd work on the docks bailing up scrap paper.

Now there was money. I liked to be well turned out and I'd be down Carnaby Street, spending a vast amount on clothes: very good trousers and beautiful imported shirts that cost over £70 even then. I don't spend that much even now and this was the eighties! And I would be out four nights a week clubbing and drinking – a pretty high lifestyle for an apprentice.

Nevertheless, by the time I reached eighteen, I was

getting fed up with the life. I began to skip the college days and instead would go to the pubs around the docks that stayed open all day and which had a complete nightclub atmosphere. One day my friend said to me: 'Bugger this, let's go to Spain!' Why not, I thought, and gave in my notice.

Unfortunately, the firm discovered I'd been skipping college and they withheld from my final paycheque the money they'd paid me for those days. I went crazy. The office was on the third floor and I started throwing all the equipment I could lay my hands on through the window. I was lucky not to hurt anyone, not least the boss. I was crying my eyes out, blaming them for cheating me and behaving very badly round the office. Now, thanks to the twelve-step programme of Alcoholics Anonymous, I realise that this shifting of blame from me to them is a common failing: they'd done nothing wrong and I was lucky to get away with my violence.

Off to Sunny, Sunny Spain

We caught the Magic Bus all the way to Lloret de Mar on the Costa Brava and stayed there for two years, only going home for parts of winter. I took up DJ-ing again and quickly got work, even as the main attraction for two new clubs that were opening. I managed to get a work permit which wasn't easy and rent a really beautiful apartment. I met a girl who lived near me in England and was quickly in love so followed

Me and my best friend Danny by the pool in our first year in Llorret de Mar

Me, Danny and Howard working at Bumpers night club in Llorret de Mar

her home. But the old feelings came back and, although I pulled up outside her house, I was afraid to knock on her door. I met her years later and she told me: 'I waited for you. I always thought you'd come and look me up.'

Next stop was Mallorca. This time it was a two-week holiday with 12 mates, all fellow West Ham supporters. On arriving at our resort we bumped into nearly 100 more West Ham fans who we knew from Upton Park, West Ham's ground. There was some appalling fighting against rival supporters. Despite this trouble, I met my future wife there who was on holiday with her friends and, when we both got home, we started seeing each other regularly. Eventually we got married and had three children – Natalie, Charlie and Harry. The wedding was a big occasion with 200 guests, horse-drawn carriages and then off to Kenya on honeymoon the following day.

Me and my mates on a beach in Magaluf with a Newcastle shirt we had taken from a supporter during a fight

IT'S NOT TOO LATE TO BE GREAT!

Married Life

My sister's husband told me he was doing the Knowledge to become a London taxi driver. I thought: I wouldn't mind doing that! So got myself an early morning job as a milkman and learnt the Knowledge in the afternoon. Money was still tight so, in the evening, I did some mini cabbing. We had our eyes on buying a new house in south-east London, but I was struggling to get the last bit of the deposit. One evening while I was mini cabbing I was telling my plight to a customer. He informed me he was the architect for the development where I wanted to buy. He gave me his card and told me to call the builder and I would be given £500 towards my deposit. Happy days! That was my deposit done. Eighteen months later I passed my Knowledge and became a London taxi driver. Things were looking up.

So there I was, a young father of twenty-two, earning good money and living in south-east London which I didn't know well. But I didn't behave. I would explain to my wife that I had no mates around there and so had to go back to the East End to drink and this meant I would have to stay over as it was too far to get back. What an excuse! In truth it meant I could drink freely, though often ending up with people I didn't know or like, in places that were seedy and dangerous. Even so if it was a choice of these dubious people with more drink and drugs or my loving family, unfortunately, I would always choose the latter.

My daughter Natalie in front of our first house we bought in South London

My wife went to college to become a hairdresser and so we bought a shop for her to set up for herself as soon as she qualified. This cost four times more than we'd paid for our house but it had a flat above, so we moved into that and rented out our house.

Things were again going very well indeed. Then my mother died and the funeral showed how much she was loved. My father had dementia and suddenly I felt very anxious again and I was deeply unhappy. My drinking and drug-taking started to spiral out of control and I was getting paranoid about the tax man and whether or not I'd been honest about my tax returns. I started worrying that my children – three of them by then – would be killed. I decided they couldn't be left and so, with my wife working in the shop downstairs, I would stay at home with them in the flat – drinking and not earning by driving my cab. To make things worse, I'd go out at night clubbing, places like Stringfellows.

Very quickly the shop was repossessed and then the house and suddenly we were homeless. I became very depressed. I expect the depression had started earlier – perhaps with the death of my mum – but it was more obvious now and I was seeing a psychiatrist but I also got heavily into drugs.

We were lucky enough to be rehoused quite quickly in a large old house in Greenwich. I had sickness insurance and so claimed that as well as my Social Security and, despite the depression, I was living a life of Riley in terms of drink and drugs and so on. The house was never going to be permanent and, after three years, we were rehoused in Eltham, to a nice maisonette on an estate, with a garden for the kids and everything around that I'd enjoyed as a child.

I'd started back driving again and one day I was in the cab with a friend when I got a phone-call with a suggestion that I help out with the movement of drugs, using my taxi as a cover. This is not uncommon in London: taxis are a good front for this sort of thing. It was a big decision: I knew that involvement in drugs carried a large sentence, but I agreed anyway.

After a while we were given the right to buy the Eltham place. I was really in the money but, however much I earned, I spent slightly more, especially on alcohol, and I would stay out three or four nights a week. At the same time, I was somehow pretty good at being a dad and my children were doing well at school! My daughter had her horse-riding and I took the boys to football. We had good breaks at Clacton in a caravan with all the cousins and we'd take holidays in Spain. I was a trainer for kids at the local boxing club and we'd go on tour with them to France. I guess I thought I was doing all right.

Our friends were also making money, but they accumulated it and I just spent it. Eventually we lost our friends too as they no longer wanted to be associated with a psycho like me. Very understandable. My wife was totally against drugs and was heartbroken by what was happening to me and to us.

I lost so much money and became bankrupt again. Luckily the house was in my wife's name, not mine, but I forged her signature and took a great slab of the equity.

I'd wanted to be great and I thought I was! But drink and drugs had taken over my life, I'd gone from twelve stone to twenty-three stone, my blood pressure was sky high, and I was bankrupt yet again. Things were very, very bad and I certainly wasn't doing anything 'great'.

3

THE DOWNWARD SLIDE

My elder brother died. He'd had a sad life. When he was a teenager, he'd been badly burnt in a fire at our house, trying to get the rest of us out. He and his wife couldn't have children and they'd missed out on adoption. He was seriously alcoholic and lost everything through it – big house, lovely lifestyle – so he lived in his holiday home. He developed lung cancer and died shortly before my other two older sisters died, also with cancer.

I'd more or less finished with driving a cab at the time. In fact, I'd bought a jewellers and pawnbrokers in Whitechapel. It really was a front, dealing with quite large amounts of money from drugs and so forth.

Unaware of what was going on, I'd been grassed up and was on police surveillance for quite some time. But, very luckily for me, they came for me just too late – If they'd come the day before I might have got twenty years! My wife was remarkably supportive because they did nick me, but just for having a small amount of marijuana, for 'personal use'. I was a very lucky man!

I was always trying to break the habit – always – both of the drink and the drugs. What this experience did was lead me to decide I'd like to be free of all that. My daughter was about fourteen and my sons around nine and it was time to be straight. I took up walking and I'd wander along with my headphones on. One day I was listening to someone talking about the way forward when the sun came out and I had something I now realise was a spiritual awakening. The sunlight suddenly burst through the clouds and I felt like God was there.

I said: 'God come into my life; come into my life.' And I believe he did. I stopped the drugs at once, and got rid of all my phone numbers. That part of my life was over, I thought, though I still had a few drinks. I went back to driving taxis and pulled away from everyone, moving to a little flat on my own we'd rented in Chislehurst, and feeling quite good.

After a year free of coke I met a friend of mine and he suggested we have a bit of gear, meaning cocaine. From that one meeting I smoked cocaine for the next five years or more, while I was driving the cab. On the way home I'd buy bottles of vodka and drink it straight – every evening. My wife never realised I was on the coke; she just thought I had an occasional puff of marijuana, which she did.

The bills were mounting up. When I'd left the jeweller's I'd owed a lot of money – many thousands of pounds – to people who had to be paid. I went to see my friend and told him about it and he paid off the debt for me. He asked me to pay him back through driving the cab, and he would match whatever I paid: when I paid £500, he would do the same. With so much generosity, that debt was paid off almost within a year! But my addiction was still out of hand; I was still sniffing and smoking cocaine. I'd be taking the boys to football in the cab, and I'd be smoking with them there in the back.

'What's that smell,' they'd ask me.

'Oh, nothing!' I'd say. 'Just the fumes from London.'

Things were getting out of hand and I started stealing from my wife's credit cards and cash machines.

'You're doing well!' she said, thinking I was working hard and saving. When she found out about the credit cards then that was it. 'I've had enough,' she told me. 'I don't think you've ever really loved me. Perhaps you married me just because I was pregnant.'

I said: 'You're probably right. I loved the dog more than I loved you.'

She looked puzzled: 'But we haven't got a dog.'

'Exactly', I replied. That was a really stupid, nasty, horrible thing to say. But what I thought at once was: Good! I'll get half the money from the house and won't have you telling me that I can't drink. The house sold fast and I got my share, although the place was in her name.

Me with my friend Terry and my two sons at my jewellers' shop in Whitechape

4

THE DARK, DARK PLACE – AND LIGHT

It was 2006. We got divorced and she met someone else. I paid her an allowance for the children and I went back to live with my aunt on the very same estate I'd grown up on. I was flash – bought myself a Rolex, lost a bit of weight, dated some girls, felt great. With one of them, we went to Dubai and Mexico and then off to Spain for the summer with the kids and their mates. But in Marbella the madness really hit me: drink and drugs and then I started to hit the whorehouses.

I sold my watch out there and some nights I was like a man possessed. Other times I'd cook the kids their meal and enjoy time with them, but within nine months of selling the house, I'd spent the lot – all the house money – and I was back in debt.

After about a month, my boys rang me to say my ex-wife's fellow had moved in and asked if they could come to me. I moved closer to them but I realised they needed to be with me. A friend offered me his other house and the boys moved there and were with me for the next four years. I wasn't touching drugs then, but I was still drinking a lot. I was driving the cab, and paid the rent and a cleaner, but never went out or socialised with anyone. My friends from younger days had all moved to Essex. I just wanted to sit indoors drinking vodka.

When they'd lived with me, my boys had wanted a dog, so we got one and he's still here with me. I have no doubt he saved my life because he got me up every single morning and I made some really nice mates of old guys with their dogs in the park. I really enjoyed it. I'd do that for two hours, then drive my cab; buy my bottles of vodka and wine on the way home and drink it all night. All I really wanted to do was drink. My weight rocketed again. It was Groundhog Day every single day.

I got to the stage where I couldn't even live like that anymore. There had been a slight recession; my rent had gone up; the cab was £1000 a month. Plus all the other bills. I rented a cab from the guy whose house I was in and it broke down. I blamed him and we argued and I said: 'Fuck it! You can have the cab back and I'm moving out of your house as well!'

My sons bought their own house and I moved in with them. They gave me money to go to a hypnotist in Harley Street to try to cure my drinking. I was sober for a few months and met a woman on Facebook, Leigh Ann, whom

I'd known from our family's holiday caravans. She was lovely and I stayed with her for three years.

One night I'd been at a wedding and got really badly drunk and did some drugs. I got home in the morning and took the dog out. There in the park I saw the Grim Reaper. I didn't have any doubt that it was him I was looking at and I was terrified. Leigh Ann told me to get to the doctor. I went to an NHS walk-in centre in Soho Square, saying I couldn't breathe. My blood pressure was 250 over 150! They said I should be on medication. I said I was, but if it was a choice between a prescription and a bottle of vodka, I'd buy the vodka. They sent me to Accident & Emergency who put me on medication to bring down the blood pressure.

Diagnosed with cancer

In February 2017 I lost my glasses. I saved up £100 and went to have my eyes tested to get new ones. I said: 'I've got high blood pressure so my sight's a bit funny.'

The woman looked in my eyes and said: 'You've got to go to A&E – at once!'

So I went to Moorfields A&E and the doctor told me I had a cancer in my eye – a malignant melanoma. 'Four hundred people a year get it in their eyes and you're one of them', he told me.

I phoned Leigh Ann and told her and told my son. My brother, who's a trader in the city, arranged for me to go to the London Clinic and the surgeon there said he might have to take my eye, but also told me that he'd be my surgeon at Moorfield anyway, if I didn't want to have the operation privately. So I had the operation on the NHS, followed by radiotherapy, and it was successful.

Nevertheless, there's no doubt that, at that point, I was at my very lowest. I thought my life had ended. I phoned Macmillan and the RNIB, sobbing my heart out. I always wanted to do something with my life, and now it seemed it was finished. My son, Charlie, asked me to come and live with him. I was really incapable of working and paying bills because my eyesight had deteriorated, though I drove a cab occasionally to get beer money.

My drinking was getting ridiculous again. Every day I'd wake up thinking this was the day I would stop, and I'd really believe it. I'll just pop to the shop and buy some eggs, I'd think. Today will be good, I'd think, so I'll just buy a little vodka. Before I got home, I'd decide to buy another bottle – just in case – and a little wine…

I couldn't work anymore. My son Charlie bought himself a house. One day he got concussed playing football and I went with him to A&E at eleven in the morning. The doctors there were more concerned with me than with him, because I was so drunk, and he told me I had to live with him. So I moved to his house and I cut my drinking right down except when he wasn't there, started losing weight, and dated a beautiful girl. I was driving again, in love, and we began having some rich old times: driving a cab in London you can earn nothing if you don't work, or a good living if you work hard!

I had a very nice time with this new girl – living the high life, staying at the Shard, all that sort of thing – but I began building up various resentments and I was drunk most of the time. We were only together six weeks. I got very jealous of my girlfriend's ex who was a dealer, and went after him, wanting to kill him. I'd always been a bit violent, but now I was absolutely off my trolley. People must have been very worried about me because my brother's friend said I should go and see his psychologist.

So I began seeing my psychiatrist in Harley Street for my violence rather than for my drinking. He used to give me these little tests. He'd say: 'Don't drink tonight and let me know in the morning how you got on.' Well, I didn't get on well! But I'd think, who does he think he is, telling me not to drink!

I'd say to my psychiatrist: 'I do my best thinking when I'm drinking.' Such rubbish: I did very little thinking, but so many embarrassing things. I loved to strip naked and I even did that at my niece's Greek wedding. All that stopped only because people didn't invite me anymore.

I got back with Leigh Ann, but it wasn't the same as it had been before and I broke with her really horribly – said all sorts of nasty things for which I'm truly sorry.

After a while of seeing the psychologist, I began to resent

paying out the money each time and I said I was leaving.

He said, 'Well, I've been meaning to say something to you.'

'What's that then?' I asked.

'You're an alcoholic! You need to go to AA,' he told me.

Well, my wife had tried to get me into Alcoholics Anonymous for years and I'd think, bless her, she must be ill if she thinks I've got a problem.

He told me: 'I've got a suggestion. If it's a choice between getting into your cab to earn some money or getting to a meeting, get yourself to the meeting. It doesn't matter about losing fifty quid.'

So I went home and looked up AA and found a meeting about 300 yards away, on a Monday lunchtime! And I went to it.

This was the turning point for me. As I write now, I want to say that honesty is key in AA and key in my recovery. So I do want to be honest, looking back on my life as I've done up to this point. My family was good, apart from having me in it. I was violent for much of my life. My mother had said to me: 'We're not that sort of family', and that broke my heart. Perhaps if she'd lived, I wouldn't have got into so much trouble.

I was a bad boy, for sure. I was extreme in every way. I wasn't nice. But when I was in that flat on my own, I was in the darkest place you could imagine: a dark room, paranoid, worried about every penny, sobbing. It was a very, very horrible life that I'd been living.

5
LIFE IN AA

When I started with Alcoholics Anonymous, I thought I would learn that I was this person who drank all the time and was so bad to people only because of the things that had happened to me: losing a finger, having my kids too young, losing my parents, and so on. All good excuses, I thought. But it was only when I did the AA programme that I realised I was selfish, self-centred and self-pitying when I didn't get my way, plus I was filled with so many character defects it was unbelievable. To stop the madness that was going around in my head, I would drink, but that first drink would create what we call 'the phenomenon of craving.' Put simply: when I have one drink I want more and I won't stop until I pass out or can't find any more.

My first meeting was held just along the road from where I was living with Charlie. It was a small meeting, usually with just eight or so people. My overall feeling of that meeting was one of hope and perhaps this is what may save my life.

However, there was one chap there who had been sober for 25 years and yet was so filled with anger and resentment that I thought: if I turn out like him, I may as well keep drinking. Luckily for me the other people there were filled with love and compassion.

People told me to get to as many meetings as possible and to find a sponsor who's armed with the facts about the 12-step program, and who can help me through it. I felt so happy talking to the other members of the meeting that I decided to celebrate. It was just after lunch and my son wouldn't be back until six, so I bought two bottles of vodka and two bottles of wine. When I got home, I fetched my pint glass and filled it with ice, vodka and a little orange, and downed it as normal.

I couldn't believe it. It tasted just like battery acid. I knew that taste because as a child I'd touched the caravan battery and then licked my fingers and the taste was terrible. I tried another pint, thinking maybe something had been left in the glass, but that one was just the same. The glass fell over and ice spread across the bed.

'For fuck's sake, God!' I shouted. 'Please, please help me.' I fell to my knees and almost lost consciousness. When I came round, I found I had an extraordinary clarity in my mind. I poured the vodka and wine away and put the bottles in the bin.

'I'm done!' I thought.

I've never drunk since, nor taken any drugs. My whole, terrible obsession to blot things out had gone.

IT'S NOT TOO LATE TO BE GREAT!

Small miracles

I was attending meetings and working through the programme, still living at my son's. He had got into a fracas and, as a result, pleaded guilty to violence and was imprisoned. His house had to be rented and so I had to go, which meant I would be homeless. My sister rang me and said I could live with her. She knew I'd joined AA.

I was still driving the taxi. Because of geography and other things, I didn't have a sponsor that I felt was right for me – someone who had a way of life that I could aspire to, with the fairness and honesty that AA talks about.

The whole structure of the AA programme of recovery is the Twelve Steps and you really do need to work through them with a man or woman you trust. I was working on the steps on my own and thinking about Step 1 and how I was 'powerless over alcohol and my life was unmanageable'.

I was living in Essex, but I went to a meeting sometimes in London. There was a man there who I'd heard talk before at a meeting and who I thought had the right ideas. I asked him to sponsor me and he agreed.

'Are you prepared to go to any lengths for your recovery?' He asked, and I said I was. 'And would you pass this message on when you've recovered?' And I said I would. 'Then it will be a pleasure,' he told me.

We started going through the Steps again from the beginning and I'd attend a couple of home meetings in

Plumstead each week. He was generous with his time and even, when I needed it, with his money. That first time I went round his house he was asking about me and my life, and I mentioned my grandchildren and named two of them: Grace and Freddie.

'Do you have a daughter called Natalie?' he asked. I was very surprised, because I do. 'If you'd come a little earlier, you'd have met them all because they came round to the house. Your daughter and my wife's daughter are best mates!' This was just incredible – almost impossible for me to believe that it was just a coincidence.

These wondrous things continue to happen to me. In one of my meditations I asked God where I could go that I would be of more use to people, especially to still suffering alcoholics. I've always had a thing about being near the sea and one day I was telling this to a friend of my son's. A man came up behind him in the shop, overheard me and said: 'Do you want to rent my caravan?' It was almost new and right on the sea.

I was still working miles away and the caravan wasn't cheap, but I took it up. My sister thought I was mad, but I knew I needed to go. In the next-door caravan was a lovely lady who looked after my dog all day.

I had some of my most spiritual moments there: walking along the seafront with the dog for miles, never mind the weather. I could feel the power of God in me and it lit me up. I'd drive off to work, attend a meeting while I was there, come back, walk the dog... I started to attend meetings local to me in Gillingham and, before I knew it, I was asked to run one of them. I was only about four months sober, but they had no one else and so I did it.

Not long after that I began to sponsor someone myself and we're still together three years later and he's still sober and we're best friends. I'd gone through the steps in a few months, and knew I was closer to God. I'd gone through the wreckage of my past, making amends wherever I could. On a daily basis the first thing I do in the morning is I pray and meditate. Throughout the day I focus on being quick to see wherever I'm wrong and to apologise swiftly. I pray anytime I'm feeling agitated or fearful and, if it persists, I phone a newcomer or my sponsor to share what's happened and this takes all the heat out of the situation. The longer I'm in AA, the less trouble I seem to get into.

The warmer weather was approaching and I was going to have to give up the caravan. I asked the local authority if they could house me. I was told that the best I could hope for was a half-way house which worried me. My sponsor said: 'Nicky, just keep working the programme. Don't worry about the money – it will sort itself out.' I would go to a dozen meetings a week and I was sponsoring people as well. I used to pray to God, just for more help so I could go and help others.

Just as my sponsor had told me, by doing all this my needs were met. Instead of a halfway house, I was offered my present home which is ideal for me and for my dog, and I can manage the rent. I had almost no furniture, but it was a good place.

Around this time I had to go for a medical to keep my taxi-driving licence. I'd had one at fifty and this was the one at fifty-six. I had to tell them about my eye problem and also, I still had quite high blood pressure, so I failed the medical. There was nothing I could do about it – I wasn't going to get a fake eyesight test, which I could have done. So, after thirty-three years of driving a taxi, I had to hand in my licence.

This was very upsetting to me after so many years and I found I'd keep getting bouts of depression: is this what my life has come to? One day, I went to the doctors about my blood pressure and in the waiting-room there was a young chap who clearly had something wrong. I had a chat and a joke with him. He was with two carers, and one said: 'You get on really well with your psychiatrist. We are looking for people at the place where he lives, so why don't you apply?'

The carers worked with people with autism. I filled in a lot of ridiculously long, complicated forms with great difficulty, having worked just for myself for years and so not ever faced anything like that. My sponsor said: 'Just fill them in, and God will sort it out – you have to meet him half-way. He can't fill them in for you!'

At this point I literally had no money at all and my sister sent me £30. I was helping a lot of people and my mobile phone was taking all my food money! I went to the food bank and, as I walked out, my phone rang. It was the Trust offering me the job, to start at the end of the month. I said, 'I'll not wait till the end of the month; I'll start Monday!'

My life has turned around

Now I work fifty yards from where I live. It's one of the most beautiful places you could imagine. Near the river and marina, I walk my dog through the woods. I'm close to a great many meetings. I'm working where I can be of use and I really love the residents and the staff. People helped me furnish my flat and my daughter gave me an old car.

God's given me so much. He needs me here because I hadn't – and probably still haven't – learnt my lessons. The trouble with God is that he puts wonderful things into your life, but he also takes things out of your life! And he doesn't give you the blueprint, so sometimes I still feel all at sea. But I stick to the programme and to my prayers, and I realise and trust it will be all right.

I've learnt so much here. For example, when I got upset at losing my taxi licence, I started to realise that this was God saying: 'I don't want you driving that cab anymore. You're not going to change doing that. You can do something better than being an angry, horrible cabdriver! You're going to work with autistic people and get a bit more humility in your life.'

Bruno

Climbing the O2 Arena

Visiting Bodmin prison in Cornwall on holiday

Inside Bodmin priso

6

THE STEPS TO FEELING GREAT

The heart of AA's program of personal recovery is contained in Twelve Steps. Along with *The Big Book*, they describe the experiences of the earliest members of the Society and others and millions around the world have turned their lives around using them, alongside the fellowship of Alcoholics Anonymous meetings. This chapter describes the ways I used them on my route to recovery.

Step 1: We admitted we were powerless over alcohol - that our lives had become unmanageable.

I never knew I was powerless; I just drank. What I did know was the aftermath of my drinking: I couldn't manage anything. I couldn't manage to go to work; I couldn't manage the bills; I couldn't manage relationships. Every area of my life was unmanageable. As a result, people in my family and friends had given me shelter, food and looked after me. Others had left me.

In terms of 'powerlessness, I gradually realised that I had never made a decision in my drinking to have that drink. It wasn't like that. I would go into a shop with all the good intentions in the world, just to pick up a can of Coke and a chocolate bar, but, as I was paying for that, out would come: 'And can I have two bottles of vodka, and a bottle of wine.'

It was only later by going through the Big Book, that I realised that, at that moment, I was actually insane. I'm purchasing something that will lead to the destruction of everything I hold dear, and ultimately to my death. Looking to the past, alcohol had made me bankrupt, got me arrested by the police, destroyed my relationship – and yet I was still making excuses to go to that shop and buy that drink. At that moment I must have been insane. Thinking about these things that had happened to me – even those that had happened the day before – was of no consequence to me at that moment. The power to say 'No' had gone. I was truly powerless.

Recognising that is the most important step of all. The first few chapters of the Big Book helped me gradually recognise this powerlessness. It's not easy to realise you're insane, but to keep doing what you're doing and think you'll get a different result – that's insane!

1. We admitted we were powerless over alcohol - that our lives had become unmanageable.
2. Came to believe that a Power greater than ourselves could restore us to sanity.
3. Made a decision to turn our will and our lives over to the care of God as we understood Him.
4. Made a searching and fearless moral inventory of ourselves.
5. Admitted to God, to ourselves and to another human being the exact nature of our wrongs.
6. Were entirely ready to have God remove all these defects of character.
7. Humbly asked Him to remove our shortcomings.
8. Made a list of all persons we had harmed, and became willing to make amends to them all.
9. Made direct amends to such people wherever possible, except when to do so would injure them or others.
10. Continued to take personal inventory and when we were wrong promptly admitted it.
11. Sought through prayer and meditation to improve our conscious contact with God as we understood Him, praying only for knowledge of His will for us and the power to carry that out.
12. Having had a spiritual awakening as the result of these steps, we tried to carry this message to alcoholics and to practice these principles in all our affairs.

Step 2: Came to believe that a Power greater than ourselves could restore us to sanity.

This was inviting me to look for this power, but with the implication that I was actually insane! This was preparing me for the next really big step: Step 3.

Step 3: Made a decision to turn our will and our lives over to the care of God as we understood Him.

I had to make a decision to make my life none of my business. That's when and where it all happens. The Third Step Prayer is really important. It meant I had to do God's will, not mine; and it says to do this would relieve me of the bondage of self, but only so I could do God's will better. Then it asks to take away my difficulties, but only once I make it none of my business.

That made me realise all the extraordinary events that led me here; not showing me the blueprint of what to do next, but just trusting him to lead me, to trust God enough that whatever he has in store for me is far better than anything I could do for myself. I turned my will over to God. If ever I start taking my will back, thinking I know better, I'm straight back into feeling bad, the old sense of 'not rightness'.

I find God deep down within me and my conception of

him is all loving and caring. He'll love me anyway, whether I drink or not. He'll always be there for me but, when I do God's will, things have worked out for me. I'm not alone. I'm at peace because I haven't got to run the show. That's wonderful!

The Third Step Prayer

God, I offer myself to Thee -
To build with me
and to do with me as Thou wilt.
Relieve me of the bondage of self,
that I may better do Thy will.
Take away my difficulties,
that victory over them may bear witness to those
I would help of Thy Power,
Thy Love, and Thy Way of life.
May I do Thy will always!

IT'S NOT TOO LATE TO BE GREAT!

Step 4: Made a searching and fearless moral inventory of ourselves.

Wow! This is a difficult one. People often stop at this: they have to do some real work on this one, and it's very soul-searching, especially as it asks you to say what part of that event was down to you – where were you to blame? For example, if something awful was done to you as a child, you're not to blame for that, of course; but, if you carry the fury from that event around with you all your life and it hurts other people, then that is your fault.

Confession is an important part of many religions and to some extent is also an aspect of psychotherapy. This step asks us to recognise which part of ourselves was hurt: our pride? our ambition? our finances? Where were we to blame? Where were we self-seeking or dishonest? Research begun in the eighties by Professor Pennebacker and others has shown the psychological and even physical healing that derives from writing or speaking about emotional events of the past. Perhaps this exercise asked of us by Step 4 offers us a similar form of healing. Honestly reporting wrongs done by us is as important as talking about the ways we have been hurt.

Doing this step was the most releasing thing I've ever done. I realised, and said, that I was to blame for everything that had happened to me. I wasn't any longer looking for a scapegoat: it was down to me. All of it. When my wife left me, it was down to me – she lasted twenty-five years with me doing wrong by her. Imagine what I'd have done if it had been the other way round, even once!

Step 5: Admitted to God, to ourselves and to another human being the exact nature of our wrongs.

After I'd written down all that inventory of my wrongs in Step 4, I sat down with my sponsor and we went through it all: the many times I was to blame. It was very easy to see that I had been selfish, self-centred, self-pitying, bullying, dishonest, inconsiderate… A total disregard of others. I'd aroused bitterness, jealousy and anger in others. I might have ruined their lives, but I'd thought: 'They deserved that!' – however small was the act they'd done to me. They might have trodden on my toe in the pub, and I'd want to kill them!

I felt such great relief after this – a great burden had been lifted off my shoulders.

When I've been a sponsor, working with someone in this way, we usually go somewhere serene to do it and it can take a long, long time. I've sat for twelve hours even to hear someone going through it all.

Step 6: Were entirely ready to have God remove all these defects of character.

Step 7: Humbly asked Him to remove our shortcomings.

These two steps are very like Step 2 in many ways. So, my sponsor and I have found all my defects and shortcomings – found I suffer from jealousy, I'm inconsiderate, and so on – and now I'm saying: God, I'm ready. I sat alone to do this; I meditated and went over them and asked God to take them away. So now I'm going to be free of all these defects because of God – maybe!

Step 8: Made a list of all persons we had harmed, and became willing to make amends to them all.

IT'S NOT TOO LATE TO BE GREAT!

Step 9: Made direct amends to such people wherever possible, except when to do so would injure them or others.

So, I had my list from Step 4, and I had to try to make amends. With my wife, I told her what a bad husband I'd been. I didn't want to tell her things that would hurt her more than I had done already. I've tried to be useful to her, but I had to be careful. I'd hurt people physically and I tried to find them, but I had no idea where they were. I told Leigh Anne how sorry I'd been for all the mental abuse I'd heaped on her, so sometimes she'd been in fear of her life. I think my kids are just glad that their dad, once such a drunk, is now helping people, and works with autistic people, and is good to his word. I hope that helps to make amends to them.

I had to pay back any money I owed, so I made financial amends to places I'd lived and not paid the council tax at various times, and to the Inland Revenue. I made a repayment schedule for various outstanding fines. I made amends to a family where I'd done wrong to one of them. Some people let me off thousands of pounds, but I was willing to repay it had they not done so. I arranged to send £35 a month to pay back the Inland Revenue, and the month I sent off the first payment I got a letter from my phone company to say my monthly bill had reduced by £35 a month! That has happened a few times: each time I made amends, God gave me the money.

I once sponsored a man who didn't want to make amends to his sister. I said, you have to do that. The Step 9 promises don't happen unless you make amends or are at least willing to do it. He asked if he could just write her a letter, and I agreed. So he wrote a letter and gave it to his mother and father and they passed it on. A week later he got a letter from his sister, thanking him and telling him she had terminal cancer. Till she died months later he became the best brother and uncle anyone could be – for her and her children. That's what comes of this wonderful programme, from God.

IT'S NOT TOO LATE TO BE GREAT!

The Step 9 Promise

If we are painstaking about this phase of our development we will be amazed before we are halfway through, we are going to know a new freedom and a new happiness. We will not regret the past nor wish to shut the door on it. We will comprehend the word serenity and we will know peace. No matter how far down the scale we have gone, we will see how our experience can benefit others. That feeling of uselessness and self-pity will disappear. We will lose interest in selfish things and gain interest in our fellows; self-seeking will slip away; and our whole attitude and outlook upon life will change. Fear of people and economic insecurity will leave us. We will intuitively know how to handle situations which used to baffle us. We will suddenly realize that God is doing for us what we could not do for ourselves. Are these

Step 10: Continued to take personal inventory and when we were wrong promptly admitted it.

Step 11: Sought through prayer and meditation to improve our conscious contact with God as we understood Him, praying only for knowledge of His will for us and the power to carry that out.

Step 12: Having had a spiritual awakening as the result of these steps, we tried to carry this message to alcoholics and to practise these principles in all our affairs.

I've turned my life around in so many ways, but can God trust me? Well, just in case he doesn't totally do so, we have Step 10. I go around every day making mistakes – not as many as I used to, not as angry as I was – but I have to continue to take care that I apply the Steps to anything I do wrong. I got a parking ticket the other day and I told the parking attendant what I thought of him. For the next twenty-four hours I hunted for him, and finally I found him.

I said: 'Excuse me, I want to talk to you.' He looked petrified, but I said: 'I'm sorry I said those nasty things yesterday, and I want to apologise. You were only doing your job. I'm sorry.'

'Thank you very much,' he said.

That made both of us feel good. So, Step 10 is another way to make me feel better. We're not after perfection – just progress. Doing this inventory each evening, looking back on the day and recognising what I'm grateful for is very helpful. In fact, I do it minute by minute through the day as well. Doing this improves my life!

I even feel grateful that I had cancer. If that hadn't happened, I might still be drinking, been homeless, trying to drive a taxi, often insane, and even without friends. It was a step towards changing my life.

I also follow Step 11 each day. This boy from Bow, involved in all sorts of silliness, who only used to pray in a police cell hoping not to be charged, this boy now gets to his knees every morning and prays for as long as his middle-aged knees will hold him. I also pray through the day if I feel agitated or angry. If I'm still not feeling right, I go and help someone, phone up a newcomer and ask how his day's been. All that has become a natural design for living for me – so much better than the life I've had before. If I've been a nice guy by the end of the day, that's enough for me.

I'm living now with integrity, tolerance, love, compassion – they make me feel God all around me. My reward for that is Step 12.

Step 12 is God's promise to us. It's all about giving.

IT'S NOT TOO LATE TO BE GREAT!

Now, in all my affairs I must take these messages to other alcoholics. I go to every prison in Kent. I try to reach one person in every meeting. Honestly, I've had a lot of buzzes in my life from all the drinks and all the drugs, but nothing has given me a bigger buzz than helping someone to go through this programme, to achieve sobriety and then they pass it on to someone else.

To see a family of fellowship grow up around me – at that moment I'm truly at one with God. I feel that my whole reason for being on earth –something I always desperately wanted to feel when I had that glass of vodka in my hand, but which it never ever did – was to do God's work. Right now, I feel the passion come into me, just thinking of this wonderful programme and what it's given me.

I always wanted that passion in my life and, at 55 at that first meeting at AA, I felt it for the first time, and that I belonged. I love to experience the warmth and love at those meetings, and knowing I belong there. They say: faith without works is dead. How true that is! The 12 Step program is a program of action and change. Just going to meetings is not good enough – we have to do more. God Bless You and hopefully we shall meet in those rooms where hope and miracles happen.

My grandchildren and my sister's grandchildren at Christmas 2021

After 50 years of great friendship, Danny and I remain close friends. Boxing Day 2021

Me with two of my loves: the 12-step programme and West Ham United

Family photo of me with my two sons, Harry and Charlie, and my daughter Natalie on Boxing Day 2021

Me with my grandchildren. (From left to right) Grace (11), Tiggy (5), Freddie (9), Woody (3) and Dusty Blue (9 months)

Me at Minnis Bay in Kent (2021)

Story Terrace

Printed in Great Britain
by Amazon